A GLANCE IN MY HEART

Can You Relate To Being Chosen?

By: Delicia Hughes

Copyright © 2024 by Delicia

Published by Deedee's Books Inc

All rights reserved. No part of this publication may be reproduced, distributed, or transmitted in any form or by any means, including photocopying, recording, or other electronic or mechanical methods, without the prior written permission of the publisher, except in the case of brief quotations embodied in critical reviews and certain other noncommercial uses permitted by copyright law.

For permissions, contact:
deliciahughesbooks@gmail.com

Table of Contents

I Picked Up a Pencil 7

Because of you 12

You 14

Letter to My Grandfather 18

Do You Really Have Friends? 23

You Don't Know Me 28

I am a woman 33

As they slept 39

I prayed. 43

What is Rain? 45

Abandoned 48

Therapy 53

War 57

Choice 60

I missed my mark. 62

Bloodline 64

Mercy 68

Faith 69

Don't Get Comfortable 71

Speak to Me 75

A Prophets Cry 78

Calling on my life 81

Synopsis: 85

I Picked Up a Pencil

I picked up a pencil and the words began to flow out of my belly. I wrote everything that popped into my head and gave it a sweet melody. I wrote and wrote page after page. I did not realize how deep down in my soul I had so many stories that started to unfold. I picked up a pencil and that feeling came back of the dark skin girl who sat on the doghouse every day with a poem book in her lap. I did not know if it was a dream come true or had the pencil been waiting to be picked up too.

I picked up a pencil and the words poured out, I could see the pain in my writing, I can hear the tears in my story, I can see at the end there was mercy and glory. As I wrote on the paper, I could not put it down. The more I wrote the more came out. I was a volcano erupting pouring out all over each line. I trembled with excitement because I thought I had forgotten how to write. But I remembered

I told God I am done walking by sight. He guided me inside and put the pencil in my hand. I remembered I used to say I cannot say put what I want to say in words, but the talent he gave me was how to write it all out. So, when I picked up the pencil, I could not put it down.

I normally run, cry and shout with a praise in my heart. But truth be told I put my thank you in black words on a blank sheet. I met a guy at the store that asked me my name and I could not tell him Deedee cause that name came with pain, so without a thought I told him Delicia instead but sadly so I felt the same. I wondered again when my breakthrough would happen, I just did not realize I needed to pick up my pencil and start tapping.

I sat in the house for a few weeks or more stuck in a deep dark raging spirit and mind war, but God then said just pick up your pencil instead cause enough is enough we are not in this season anymore. As I sit by myself, I have felt so alone, this whole time not knowing I am being groomed to write once again so when I started to pour out within the letters jumbled together on the lines began to be my own praise and worship song. As I wrote he reminded me how the potter started with just a clump of clay. But the potter was bold because he decided to pick it up that day.

He shaped and molded each one in its own way, I guess when I look back at the pages it is the molds from my clay. I picked up a pencil, not knowing how long I have been scared to do so, but as the flow began the spirit left and I pulled everything out from deep down within. When I picked up the pencil, I thought about David, he was ready to ride when nobody would, so I started my scribe even though nobody else even knew I could. Like fire and brimstone that rained on Sodom and Gomora, was the emotions I felt when I wrote down my horror. I told my truth, and I poured it all out. I unlocked the secrets in Pandora's box, I cannot even say that the things I said made me shocked.

I picked up a pencil and it all started with a sermon I heard that said do it from the heart. I thought about it and went into prayer that night and said God grant me sight, clear whatever it is that have me blocked. Me thinking I am praying to understand more dreams I prayed a prayer that unlocked my mind, and restored my hand, it resurrected a gift I buried, and thought was dead. When I picked up the pencil my mind was no longer blind, I could see clear as day and as I wrote in the dark there was a light that showed bright and guided every word that was printed from the point.

I have had many testimonies of how God showed up, I even seen his mercy and glory, and yes, I have witnessed his salvation, and strength. But my real testimony was the feeling I got of finally being free to say what I want to and not care what others think, the feeling I got that made the pain bleed out and stain the blank pages in my book, which gave me an inside shout, I experienced a miracle right before my eyes as the words began to make sentences, the wonderful feeling of the peace being upon me as I wrote and wrote about why has been done to me. I look back and read and just like he said. I counted it all good because leviathan was dead. I experienced a real pour out, I felt like Joseph when he brought his family to his promise land.

No, I am not a Bible scholar but I do know the stories. Like the widow's oil kept pouring and pouring that is how I described the way my hand kept going. I sat and I spent hours in a realm, where the mustard seed began to bloom, and I was not at all confused. My mind never went black, the words just kept following through. Now I can say my healing and it started with a whisper in my heart that said pick up the pencil it is time to start.

Because of you

Even though I never heard you say you love me.

I am who I am because of you.

Even though at the hands of you I gained the most scares.

I am who I am because I am you.

Even though for every happy moment you turned to trauma.

I am who I am because of you.

Even though you broke my heart first.

I am who I am because of you.

Even though you judged me first.

I am who I am because of you.

Even though you made me feel abandoned.

I am who I am because of you.

Even though I wanted to die rather than live as your slave.

I am who I am because of you.

Even though you made me insecure.

I am who I am because of you.

Even though you made me feel the worst.

I am who I am because of you.

Even though I remember more troubled times than good.

I am who I am because of you.

Even though I hated to look at myself cause I seen you.

I am who I am because of you.

Love, blood, sweat, deceit, anger, and snares.

It is a general thing and I am introducing a new era.

You

I ignored you for months and never wanted a real chance. But that night you popped up I took a second glance. I remembered your order #2 with cheese with two doubles, a sprite and made sure it was large sized. I gave you my number yet again this second time, just playing a game in my head while calling you all mine. We went out and hung out and that night you were done. But not me, I was still young and free, I had just turned eighteen so I was waiting to see what your body could do for me. I grabbed you close and gave you a strong dare, not knowing that when we were done, I could never go nowhere. After that moment of lust, spending life with you was a must, but deep down inside I just wanted to buss.

Each date we took we rode hand in hand even though while I worked you played your own game. Every woman was mad asking how was it true, they yelled with heart ache he only has love for you. So again I am thinking this love must be real, could it be time to now seal the deal. Of course, it did not work because I joined this church, and the pastor told me that this man was not mines. Instead of taking heed, I gave you a choice to never have sex with me until we were married of course. After that moment it took 3 months, by May we were engaged and planning our life. The big day came on August 26, I knew something was wrong because nothing could be fixed. My nails were done late cause on the way I wrecked my car. Still wondering should I go on, but I did because we came this far. With only two people in the room, we said our I do.

How was I supposed to know that this would change you? We had a life full of challenges that had a lot to bear and instead of seeking help you used me to release all the stress you picked up. That was when I knew I messed up. I stuck it out because a son we brought into this world even though we lost two daughters, and you never even gave me a hug. You never comforted me in my pain instead all you wanted was sex, so every night with tears in my eyes I laid there waiting for you to be done. All the hurt I was dealing with alone took away all the fun. So soon our life became just a routine and then I wondered many times when did you ever get so mean.

You made fun of my shape and the religion I took. You never even heard me or seen the emptiness inside. Not at all aware of the fact that with Delacie I died. My body was present, but my mind was long gone so I set out to again find love on my own. I met this guy who made me feel alive, and that day I told you we had to be done. But you cried to me and apologized, you promised to fix it and to be better. But the fact that I had found someone made you only keep me stuck as a get back. So, at 3 months pregnant I found out about her, I was not even mad I just knew it was complete. That was my final escape, I knew I could be free.

But you refused to leave and kept me trapped and tortured inside. So nightly I cried because I had no other guide. I was stuck in a marriage not knowing what to do. All I knew was that I had no more love for you. But once I got out, I found a new me, only to find out I still was never free. The chains of pain still held on to me strongly. I took pill after pill to sleep it all away. To find myself in a hospital with everyone asking how you get this way. But nobody knows the pressure you go through, cause when you walk back into your house and close the door it is just you.

But where I am now, I finally let go, cause deep down in my heart that is one door I know closed. So, I let it stay shut to completely be healed. I am happy with my decision, though at times I blame you for causing these scars. We can always be friends but never your wife, I married you one time and after that I know now I would never do it twice.

Letter to My Grandfather

I don't even know where to start. I never even know where to begin but for the writing sake, I'll just jump right in.

I have always admired you. For as long as I can remember. You were the very example of the perfect man I would want to leave my family. You were my hero. When we wrote about our hero in school, I always wrote about you. The strong man of the family who worked with his hands and devoted to the Lord. But for some reason I still didn't feel fully accepted by you. I loved my granddad, and I enjoyed our small talks, but I could not figure out how a man of honor, a man well respected and a man who loved his legacy could allow his first born grandchild to endure so much harm. You blamed it on Jesus and all about peace and keeping down confusion. But yet as I paid close attention you were never really there for me. You cared from a distance but never was hands on.

I've watched you complete the other kids on their games and even sit and watch them play. But yet my children don't have the support of none of y'all. I never asked you to take over being his father, I simply asked you to be a grandfather and to help me. It's taking a village to raise these children and also family support. It's a shame I had a mother and a father and yet had nobody to truly be there. You didn't even go to my graduation ceremony, and yet you still don't know that I prayed for Jesus to restore you back to health the day me and you both were hospitalized. Not once were you there for me when I went through. I admired you for so long but yet I was so wrong.

My father wasn't your real son and through me it showed. The abuse he endured at your hands wasn't always in love. But being that you are such a Bible following man how did you not know that you were evoking a generational curse. You follow the word so you say but yet the word tells you to take care of your own house first and when you married my grandmother that was the covenant you made. But instead of feeling the covenant you lacked in many areas. Your mind may be saying you right in how you lead but your heart is not leading in the God ordained direction. You have destroyed your own bloodline, and you don't even know it. I sit back and I watch just like you do. You claimed to be a fisherman but yet when you cast down your net it comes back empty. You accepted every attack the enemy placed on your household. Even the stories you and grandma buried and were never told. But you allowed the enemy to encamp around. Instead of holding to your faith and knowing the power that back you. So many things could have been stopped but you don't truly have the relationship with God to fight through your warfare. You are stuck in bondage on a religion that brought you out. However, the glory goes to God. You are faithful to the church and y'all follow so many rules that you're contradicting the rules in your own way. God says he will pour out his spirit to all flesh but you all will acknowledge only the spirit in men to rise up. I followed behind y'all and joined the church and that was the first real time you truly accepted me. When you baptized me, I wasn't happy about being saved, I was only happy that I made you happy because I've longed for that acceptance for so long. But if you read your Bible just like I do, you'll see how that was wrong because you were made my idol. So instead of y'all preaching and teaching to read the word on your own, you make the women wait to be led by a man. But God said we all need to study not just one or the other. So again, tell me how your way is so right. I learned many ways of God and the more I learn the clear things become to me. The spirits I had attached to me that tormented me so long was yet destroyed when I left and ventured out on my own. I went and built a relationship with God on my own and after that he began to set me completely free. Now of course, test and trials will always come but God said we have nothing to worry about as long as we trust in him. He who has overcame the world. Every time I came to you for help, you left me to run astray. But when you are raising up new fisher-mans you supposed to teach them the way. You tell how I don't have Jesus because I don't choose to be bound by your religion.

However, God never said he was restricted to one place. You always said Gods covering had left me. But you lied again because he said he would never leave me nor forsake me. The sad part is, had I believed your words it could have drove me into suicide but because I was stronger in my faith and knowledgeable in my word I was able to go to Jesus myself and ask him. He answered me swiftly with a response to a prayer I had prayed for years, and all I did was tell him to show me I'm in the right place. God knows my heart but it's sad you don't even know me. I am happy and I am free because I have cast all my cares upon him. I have surrendered my life to God, and I believed in Jesus and through him I shall always have peace, joy and victory. I am going to be great, and God is going to show himself so mightily in my life. He loves me so dearly and I can't wait till you see his true mercy and glory through me. This is not out of exalting myself, but for you to really see the hand of God on my life and become free by the spirit of God which lives in me.

So in the midst of my great fall, I called you for help but instead you beat me down and accused me just like my mother all my life when I was just needing help along the way. Even Simon helped Jesus carry his cross but yet you led me to shame, disbelief and heartbreak. But it's ok I don't hate you. I still admire you for being you. But I wish and I pray that one day you will finally be free from bondage too.

Do You Really Have Friends?

We meet people who we click with and vibe with. Those same people we share our secrets with and trust to have our back. However, that trust comes with stipulations that are unspoken but seen as time pass. We hang out, party and engage in underage drinking and clubbing and y'all are with me every step of the way.

Being raised up scared to sneak and do anything, this new friendship paved the way. The friendships give you a sense of comfort that allows you to open up and be what you think is really you. However, there is people who join in the mix, and you explained how they would destroy all of what you and your sisters or friends knew. You fight with the newcomers and your so-called friends find reasons as to why you are always in the wrong. But the slight shots as we called them, however, was silently bullying and always left unhandled.

Yes, when strangers around the gang stuck together but still having confusion and abuse in our own crew. A separation took place when one walked away. Started a family and started living life in a righteous way. But once that hurt came from the scars of life going wrong, you are welcomed back into the unhealthy song. So now you back partying and hanging out with the same crew who claim to love you but often leave you out. Then you look at the relationships everyone has with the kids and notice your kids are the only ones who don't experience the same love.

They think you just complaining when you began to speak out, so then you stop them from coming around because they too felt the difference and the hurt of being left out. But you continue to be there because your type of loyalty is rare. Only to ask when you homeless can you stay there. But you get a response of no, so you move on and sleep on the couch on weekends when the kids are gone. Only to see others move in and out which cause your mind to be confused, and the audacity is hard to figure out. You use a car of a loved one a sister who used that moment to pick a fight and judge you. Then you sit down and think, oh how I swear I thought I had friends that was family. But then you were treated like an outside, while the outsiders were invited right in. Often times you give warnings not to trust this person or that person, only to be discarded and later to find out you was speaking all facts. Even though it was said the love was there. You feel different cause the room becomes uncomfortable and weird just because your presence is there. Then when you try to give an encouraging word of advice you get attacked once again and the truth is then revealed. Being told that nobody likes you in the middle of the group is a tad bit hurtful when there is nobody to speak up, we do. When we yell and say y'all I'm hurt, once again everyone walks away and leave you abandoned in a place and ignored for months not even asking if you ok. Then it really sets in when you began to see, everybody loves everybody, but nobody truly cared for me. Everyone was there when your life was overtaken by misery and sin but when you were happy and submitting to God nobody supported the new decisions that came from within. It was weird and all the red flags you ignore. But God showed you many times there was snakes in your circle. But you stayed close because of the love and loyalty you had because you thought you were family. Time after time, argument after argument, you gave many chances.

Then when you explode you the one get the weird glances. But at this point you no longer see family, the only thing on your mind is that these people keep attacking me. When you accomplish something new, not many support you. Yes, some birthday parties have been accompanied however no help was ever provided. When you have made the notion to provide everybody in the group surprise parties and extend extra support during their birthdays but when yours come around nobody has the same energy and joy you provide. When you look and notice, you always provide for your own celebration then you stop and think, are these really friends. You see time and time again how everyone celebrates one another but yet you notice your celebration is missed unless you provide is mind blowing but yet becomes normal.

You accept things because of love and loyalty when you should have been walked away and kept going. It's ok to know people for half your life and see one day that they weren't for you anyway. It's ok to find out late you were surrounded by hate, the main part is knowing how to let go so you can grow. Sometimes when you can't do it on your own, God snatches you away dramatically, in order to rip off the bandage so the healing can begin. Then you notice when the healing began the blessings flow through, and you ask God to tell you what happened, and he advise that they were not anointed to go with you.

Whether it's a friendship, relationship or even family, stop holding on to something or someone who was supposed to been long gone. Through letting go, your heart be at so much peace and the Lord's blessings start to flow and never cease. Listen and take heed to the red flags given all around you, because if you ignore them, you'll find you, having to pick yourself off the ground. Love yourself and allow God to lead your way and you will love the difference in living life his way.

You Don't Know Me

You claim to know me in and out but truthfully you don't know me at all. You know the small things that you have noticed along the way, but you don't know me at all.

You may have seen that my spirit and heart is pure however you don't know me. You know a version of me that you have given me yourself by mixing the knows with mystery.

You combined the two and came up with your own version that I'm supposed to live up to.My response to your words shocks you every time because you expect me to move differently.

Sadly, to say that's your own image and notion of thinking which will allow you to be shocked every time. I look at people with a poker face is what they call it or a distance gaze. People often get offended by that stare, and it started with my own mom.

In reality the stare is me watching you yelling or speaking in anger projecting your views and values on me. When clearly, I don't see the situation, the lifestyle, or even the world the way you do. I sometimes cry because of how lost people are when they think they are telling me about me.

It's funny you see but I shed tears instead of the smirk or smile because in my heart you already lost me in the part where your way is only right.

God said he is the truth an let every man be a lie, so I lose you in the mystery of my eye. The frustration comes because people feel like I'm supposed to acknowledge their version of how they claim I feel.

When in reality the very moment you think I'm listening I'm really not. I've prayed already, God cover me from what is intended to offend me or hurt me. So, I'm protected from people's inner spirits that they don't even see.

The moments I'm listening and taking heed. The notes are mental, so I record it all and pray on my knees.

Do you know I see things about everybody I just don't speak because I know many people truly can't handle what I see in and through them. Do you know I see images while people are speaking but I stay quiet and smile and pray to myself.

Do you know the visions I see I'm constantly thinking and seeing even in my sleep. Do you know my heart was so torn at one point and because I got beat for everything I accepted hurt into my heart.

Do you since I've been healed and my likes and loves have still remained the same. Do you know I'm still me I just guard what comes in and out and who I'm around. Do you know I hear you and many others but I pay close attention to what is sound. Do you know there is a nudge that happens whenever someone lies to me so my trust is kindled because I see your deceits.

Do you know I have a journal of things untold because when I say it from my mouth people get offended. Everyone yells the same thing when I'm right. It's how you say it and not what I say but before it came out, I had already prayed that God allow it to be released in his way. When I'm standing ten toes down is because I hear my father's sound and nothing you say will make me stray away.

When I asked for my new heart, I prayed for God to never take away my spark. Truth be told I really accept people as they really are, but nobody accepts me, they genuinely don't like the person they see.

There are many times God place my spirit in a room and allow me to hear the things that are spoken and said. Even when there's a moment of silence. So when I ask questions about the simple fact other scenarios are being addressed besides full ownership of what's said. I watch the offense all over people face however I don't get offended because I already knew. The kicker is I may argue my point just for fun. Then I quickly get bored cause my battle been won. So, I watch in a daze as you do you.

Nobody knows my frustration from anger. Nobodies knows my happiness to sad. Nobody knows when I'm deep in thought. The weird part is I tell people about me from the very start. So, when the opinions form, I just observe and see how people lean on their own invented understanding of me.

I know I'm not perfect I have my own faults. I'm not always right but I don't portray to be. I am who I am, I am who I was born to be, I'm not what anyone calls me or say, I'm not someone else's image I'm simply me.

I am a woman.

Sometimes I forget to feed my kids because I have not even eaten because I was too busy running around for them.

I am a mother.

Sometimes I must tell them I'm a do it in a minute and forget all about and still get it done.

I am a mother.

I have many moments I wanted to put you on the steps and leave but I could never leave your side for nothing.

 I am a mother.

Maybe your whooping's are really that final moment when I am tired of you not caring about yourself and I can't stop caring.

I am a mother.

So many people want to watch you and keep you and I want to let them because I need a break, a nap, or a drink, maybe even a smoke. I am a mother.

I gave everyone their own beds and rooms and still all y'all sleep with me. But I do not make you get out. I simply snuggle in the corner on the edge, so you do not fall.

Cause I am a mother.

At the moment I wanted to get a passport because it was time for me to travel and be free, I just brought an extra three so they can travel with me.

I am a mother.

Instead, I keep you all to myself because I got to persevere my blessing, I got to protect my blessing, I cannot mishandle my blessing.

I am a mother.

I love to kiss the small feet, but I cannot stand the way you hum while you eat.

I am a mother.

I want to kick my feet up after a long days work, but I got to sit and watch you roll around the floor, make an experiment, mess up my kitchen, help with homework I don't even know no more, to email the teacher for an example, even though my assignment about to be past due, to listen about your day and its multiple. Cause I am a mother.

I have to spend my nights awake watching you sleep as I silently cry.

I am a mother.

I show you so much love, I do all I can do; I be extra with you cause I am extra with me.

I am a mother.

I have to hurt you and hold you to show you I love you and I care for you.

I am a mother.

Is it true? Am I the one that is causing your trauma? I am sorry but how?

I am just a mother.

I love you with parts of my heart I did not know I had, but I love me to, I love me more,

I am also a woman.

I want to sit and talk with another woman or another man.

Cause I am a woman.

I want to do my hair, gloss my lips, and smile in the mirror.

Cause I am a woman.

I want to get dressed, twirl around and pose in the mirror.

Cause I am a woman.

I want to twerk and be wild because to me being wild is free. That is what I get from Adam and Eve

Cause I am a woman.

I want to strip for my man, be gripped till our bodies infuse, and I do not want to think about none of you, but I cannot because my bed is occupied.

Does that make me a bad mother? Or just a woman?

I only want to care about myself, I only want to take care of myself, I want to be myself, but I can't care about nothing but you, whether I take care of me I make sure I take care of you, and every moment you out of my sight my breath stops, and my heart skip several beats.

 Does that make me a good mother? Or just a woman?

When I am tripping over all these toys, and listening to all this noise, all I want is for it to be quiet and clean.

Does that make me a bad mother or a woman.

I want to be Meg in May, a city girl in June, and cardi in July in all different worlds. But I prepare you for the test, take you to practice, dress you for your prom, miss an entire day at work for your 2-hour graduation, be your personal parade. Knowing I am the only one that is going to be extra cause I'm extras for me.

Does that make me a good mother? Or just a woman.

When I pray for my covering, I got to pray for yours first, because I gave you back to him even when I was not ready to be free cause I know he will love you more than me.

37

The wild thing is as one person I am both.

I am a sexy ass woman who happens to be a mother of a few amazing kids.

As they slept

As they slept, I cleaned the house.

As they slept, I took my bath.

As they slept, I did my work.

As they slept, I was his sex slave

As they slept, I was his maid.

As they slept, I felt all alone.

As they slept, I watched all entrances.

As they slept, I sat and cried.

As they slept, I asked God why.

As they slept, I died inside.

As they slept, I read Gods word.

As they slept, I shouted outside.

As they slept, I lost myself.

As they slept, I poured it all out.

As they slept, I took time for me.

So, when they woke, I was free.

Curiosity killed the cat.

Curiosity killed the cat and now I cannot get that time back. I spent years because I was curious searching to see where real love was at.

Curiosity killed the cat and now I am stuck single with three, used and abused by men who claim they loved me.

Curiosity killed the cat cause when I saw you, I was drawn, not knowing that once I got you, it would end all wrong.

Curiosity killed the cat cause when I finally said I do, I assumed that your commitment was gone be like mines but instead you never followed through.

Curiosity killed the cat because I had to prove them wrong, your ex-lover, our friends and sadly my mother. Instead, I pushed myself into a dark hole trying to be bold.

Curiosity killed the cat now fancy that, when I got pushed off the porch, I then leaped and fell on my own torch.

Curiosity killed the cat all because I wanted to know how it truly felt, to be as one and no longer two but then we got stuck cause you never grew.

Curiosity killed the cat, cause that one night I was in a daze from all the drinks that was made and what I seen was a light that looked like an angel, but it had a deep demon tucked away.

Curiosity killed the cat there is no more heart left to break, I took the pieces and laid them down and when I got up, I adjusted my crown.

Curiosity killed the cat cause now the old has become new, I sat alone telling myself you got to learn the new you.

Curiosity killed the cat but from the story I read, he made it just in time because Lazarus was not dead. So, when he said come forth, I sprung up, leaving behind my old dread.

Curiosity killed the cat, but clearly it was not my time, so I stretched my arms out wide and begged God for a sure sign.

Curiosity killed the cat, but when I fell upon the ground and called Jesus, he reminded me I've been bought back.

I prayed.

I prayed for love, a close family, a nightly kiss and a hug, someone like me, someone who would want to be around me with no strings attached.

I asked for a sprinkle of wild, so we got similar night style. I prayed hard and hard for my own army.

I wanted someone I could share the classics with. I wanted to build and grow with someone. I prayed for the physical touch. I prayed to never die alone.

Then when he answered I received love that has no measurement, I have several arms around me, not enough cheeks to take all the kisses, I was blessed with three different inseparable parts of me.

Who protects me the same I do them. He sent me a family that has movie night once a week. He gave me blessings to build and grow of my own that will in later days do the same for me.

My own legacy. More than one reason to smile. I was given his yes and Amen.

He sent him in them, so I just decided to give him the rest of me 💐🙏

What is Rain?

Looking up I see the sky is painted with a fluffy grey.

But the song writer says the sun will come out the next day.

When I look into the mirror and stare deep into my eyes.

It reminds me of those fluffy grey clouds in the skies.

Now in my head I am thinking will the sun inside shine bright tomorrow.

Or am I going to be forever tormented by this deep-down sorrow.

Looking up I see the burst of clouds pouring out the rain.

So of course, I wonder what I can do to allow an out pour of this deep dark pain.

So, from the way life works the rain comes down to make the plants grow.

Now I wonder if my pain pours out just like rain, will I be able to look in the mirror and see my eyes glow?

Watching the clouds and the rain it is so gloomy and dark.

Seems like my soul is searching for the source but does not seem to know where to start.

So, sitting here thinking how does this all work? Do the clouds fill up and burst, then rain falls?

I am trying to understand since to me I feel Like I have already burst but I don't seem to see nothing at all.

So, I am asking what exactly is rain?

Is it a downpour of all my grief and deep dark pain?

Is it just a temporary moment when the sky turns grey, and the rain comes down until tomorrow?

Then once everything is all clear and poured out that will be the end of my dark sorrow?

Let us not forget after the rain the flowers, trees and grass grow.

Which gives me hope that when my soul pours out, I will once again see my eyes glow.

Abandoned

I remember once lying beside you in bed rubbing my toes on your leg. That was the last memory I have of being that close to you.

Then you abandoned me.

I remember when we walked hand in hand on your way to work. That was the last moment I remembered being that close to you.

Then you abandoned me.

I went off to college which was a happy time for me. But I struggled with all my peers hating me. The dorms were nasty, and I always broke out in hives. I cried to come home and you said there was no room for me anymore.

You abandoned me.

You came by a few times, you brought me gifts and spent time with me. You always told me how beautiful I was and how I would always be your princess.

Then you abandoned me.

You came by to see me once more, in that visit it was real strange you backed me in a corner and tried to kiss and hug on me. Then you came running to my defense 5 years later.

Then you died and abandoned me.

You were my best friend who I cared for so deeply, but I just wanted to be your friend. You were around for my marriage and my children, but you wanted more than I was willing to give.

Then you abandoned me.

We dated for years even though it was puppy love, my heart was in with you long and strong. I hung around and loved you when life had you down. In and out my life for years you were.

Then even too you abandoned me.

You got me every weekend; you made sure I had everything I needed. You loved on me and taught me how to reach for God in every situation, then I grew up and when I moved out you carried me for a little while longer.

Then you abandoned me.

Then we reconnected on a new level in our relationship because I went to your church and began to act like you of course. But there was an unsettling deep-down unhappiness and after I loved so did your love for me.

Then you abandoned me.

Let us not talk about the kids because my kids do not know nobody, and nobody knows them. But y'all smile in the faces four times a year and whisper in their ear, the little promises that they knew were untrue.

Then y'all abandoned us.

We were friends to the end, two peas in a pod. We did everything together. This circle of life has been played a few times, it's just everyone had a season, cause once again,

They abandoned me.

I gave my heart and my love. I put the effort into giving the attention. I love hard but I refused to be led wrong. The small knowledge I had I still applied without knowing how and why.

You did not want to be the man I needed and the man you were required to be. So, in the later days you miss me.

But you abandoned me.

I carried you it seems like four different times, each time you grew, and I felt your flutters. The hunger and I felt the growing pains. I pushed you out and held y'all in my hands, I kissed your face. Your bodies go from warm to cold all in a matter of hours.

Then you abandoned me.

I prayed and I called out, some answers I never received. Then I became blind and was easily deceived. I went through torture after torture with just glimpses in small moments of peace then I was back in a world wind of lies and deceit. The biggest hurt when in my own head I felt.

That even you abandoned me.

I have been placed in the cycle of life where people come, and people go. Not just leaving me behind or taking a graceful bow out. However, people come in and scrape the half-healed wounds while creating scabs and scars of their own. Then they abandoned me. For the love of God, I could not figure out why people came in only to destroy the beauty of the person that I was created to be. Then I soon came to see that I was not yet abandoned but because of the hurt feeling in my heart when people walked out, there was a spirit of abandonment that came into me.

Then I came across the one promise that took root. To never leave me or forsake me, out of the good book. Then I looked back to see that the whole time it was not him abandoning me, but it was the choices I made that left me alone, the heart that I had that would not turn back home.

Due to my emotions, I was stuck in a generational cycle of sin that had me abandon the true God-fearing woman that was hidden within.

I am the one who abandoned me.

Therapy

I wonder how bringing up my pain will help me heal. When it is like a carousel already and makes me angrier. I remember constantly the things I have been through even though I have moved past them in my heart. I tell myself I am healed, to practice speaking it into existence. But when something happens it is like ripping off a scab. It is always a new person doing the same thing in a new way. I have forgiven my mother because I've seen her as the source, even if to me there's no real remorse. I often wonder how pouring it all out will close the open portals to my destiny that lives on the inside of me. I get so angry when a snake snakes me even if I already knew who they were. I often wonder if I tell the truth will you lock me up and call me crazy too. When I shot him, I wanted to stomp him until he was dead, are you sure it is ok to share what's in my head? Often times when I fight, I want to see the blood shed to ensure they feel the pain they have caused deep in my heart, but wait hold on this is therapy right? I often wonder what they are thinking while they sit down and write. But truth be told I really don't care cause to me right is right and wrong is wrong. But they expect us to believe that life's not supposed to be fair. I sit at the computer and answer the phones in a constant cycle of telling people they are paying for a coverage but no real protection. Instead I take down their information and transfer them to the next disappointment. But I say I want to help people, sounds like a scammer to me, but I refuse to be the tax collector. I love to drink, dance, and have sex, I loved to be pounded so hard and so deep I ended up passed out, and wake up cuddle because it feels like it all released out. but there is a specific way and order of life. The wrong move could cost you your soul. I forgot this is just therapy, are you sure you want to hear more? A human that carries their own cross got to listen to all my self-faults. When I drive over bridges, I think about just driving off, now for sure I will be in a strait jacket cause of what they call suicidal thoughts. But this is therapy do not let my thoughts scare you, remember it's your job to help me sort it all out. They must give you guided ways to make you feel sane. But deep down inside I know I am past normal; I have been shackled with invisible chains. Can you see the things attached to me? Nope you hear my story and ask me if I feel free. They must listen and be truly in-tuned, but I see you are just as drained, watching the clock, and planning dinner for the kids just like me. I love how the room Is set up to make me feel comfortable to talk. But you have no idea how those things do not work. I laughed at their pain because they cried like me, I laughed when they fall because they wished bad on me. I laughed so hard it brought tears in my eyes, but I never feel bad. So, what am I? This is therapy right let me get it all out. I signed a waiver that says it stays in this room. But we both know that's not true cause I carry every wound. Why do you scratch your head to figure me out? I have read a story that told me I let leviathan in. I pull out all the love that I carry within, cause regardless I cannot let him win. I am reminded again I was bought with a price. So, I praised and shouted to cast him and all his agents out. I guess here is the part where I have finally said something nice. This is therapy how deep can I go? Can I ask a question, how much of the Bible do you know. I wonder sometimes after I take it too far, what is all wrong with me and if it will ever stop. But this is therapy so let me talk and help me heal, but my story being told aloud is not posed to be for me. It is to save the souls that Christ assigned me to. So, I come to sit and talk to you when I was already told to look to the hills for my help. I often wonder if sometimes I do not look because it seems too far and to get to, but you are a quick drive in the car. Geesh, can I scream because my mind is sometimes scrambled. But that is the spirit called confusion. I often wonder with all the knowledge I have; how do I still make the wrong decisions? Is it my heart or my head or the curses from generations of people who are now dead? I laugh because I have been given an hour to talk. These sessions are about up and I'm nowhere near done with my thoughts.

War

Fighting this battle and this war in my heart and in my mind.

Trying hard to stay steady but I keep stumbling over the line.

We are given a measurement of mercy and a measure of grace but it's coming to a point where we're running out of time.

Believing what is ahead of you yet scared to leave certain things and people behind.

Knowing deep down God is my soul source of life and I can trust him.

Trusting fully is not the problem, yet our flesh makes us nervous about going out on a limb.

It is like having your cup so full yet you are careful not to go over the rim.

Floating in the water in a daze knowing good and well you can swim.

Wanting to get closer to God is something that has a hold on my heart.

Looking in the mirror I do not look, walk, or even act the part.

Faith is not what we see, yet what we believe which is some form of art.

Reading, writing, and thinking but still unclear on the very place to start.

After a full meal your belly is yet empty, so you try to eat snacks to satisfy that hunger.

Clearly that is not the answer so now you are here again your mind began to wonder.

It is like a feeling of emptiness that cannot be filled that came on when you were younger.

Trying to swim against the waves but somehow still getting pulled under.

Study to show yourself approved, but what does study truly mean?

I learn by just reading and seeing the words play out in my mind while I analyze every scene.

Sometimes it works and sometimes it does not so then I sit and wait on the Holy Spirit to intervene.

His presence and I began to feel full, but my understanding is still yet unseen.

As I lay down, I pray inside that the blockage in my mind is destroyed and things become clear.

Even still in the midst of the clouds I trust and believe everything will start to appear.

One thing I am sure of is that God is real, and he is yet always near.

Choice

I once heard a saying on a show, God watched His children, hearts aglow, yet disobedience and wayward paths they chose, A loving Father with two choices arose.

1. Destroy them all, and end the tale,

2. Die for them, though it would entail, A sacrifice beyond all measure, A gift of love, an eternal treasure.

Then came Jesus, gentle and true, A beacon of hope for me and you. He chose to die, our sins to bear, His life, a testament of love and care.

Now we, His children, face our own test, two choices lie within our chest.

1. Be destroyed with those who stray,

2. Die to yourself daily and follow His way.

To die to oneself is a daily fight, A journey of faith, bathed in light. Results of salvation, a soul set free, Living for Him, eternally.

So let us choose, with hearts sincere, to follow the path that brings us near. Near to His love, His grace, His light, choosing to live, in His holy sight.

I missed my mark.

God spoke to me in a parable I can only understand and told me to write it down. But I was in the middle of watching a sermon that was really good might I add.

However, I did not write it down. I immediately decided that I was gone hold the thought till I was done watching what had my attention.

But then as I sat there, I came to the revelation that God do not care about what sermon or song got you moved when he talking to you directly.

I began to think hard so I finally was like let me pause it before I lose it.

As I pulled up the document with no time for pad and pen. I held the empty screen in my hand with my mind blank.

I was you the one reading me.

Do not miss your mark!

Bloodline

Watching my son out there and just hearing this is young buck. He is tough and he is strong and fearless. To see the other coaches remember once being around my dad and seeing his grandson they see his bloodline. Looking through the inheritance that was set before him we see the strength and courage. We see the knowledge and the power he upholds. That makes us proud to be called our father's children. We often times look down on our family tree and see the different attributes that put us together. We are built off the things that run through our bloodline.

But the fact that we miss it is that it can be a blessing or a curse. When we see ourselves, we do not see the different curses like poverty, shame, anger, incest, witchcraft, non-progress and anti-marriage, and early premature death.

If town takes us to go through life to see those things exposed.

Ideally truth be told those things unfold at initial stages in life. We can see anger in a child as young as infancy just by the way he reacts to not getting his bottle right away, or even a toddler with the tantrums they throw. The world disguises those things as developmentally appropriate and gives them cute names like terrible twos. The only thing that is terrible is the fact the parents did not realize the curse that they carried and inserted in you.

Both parents filled with sin one the mother striving and fighting to do right and the other the father stuck in an endless cycle afraid to seek help and confused about how to seek God. Fear and confusion which leads to anger, frustration, and anxiety. The bloodline has been bruised and scared with the sins of our parents.

We see the child get frustrated; we see the child angry when he cannot get it right. We see the child having it hard to feeling the sense of belonging. That too was part of the spirits running rampant through the bloodline. Doors opening and doors closing not knowing what is coming in and what's coming out. But there is a mother that know she cannot live without the abundance of God's grace and mercy.

Watching the child line up on the field and stop and block the biggest players on the field. We can see how strength and resilience that was once seen in our father. The faces that he makes remind everyone of his grandfathers. But there is this knowledge that is intense, that could only be a gift from God. We see how a combination of Gods gifts that were planted in our children from the womb makes a child who they are.

We have often seen many characteristics that we have no idea where they came from which is where faith and prayer and living your life accordingly allows for you to block and destroy anything on the bloodline that came from family members before you. The bloodline does not stop as long as we have children. The same characteristics, curses and blessings are yet passed down the line.

As a parent that sits back and looks at her son, I am proud at most of the things that are intwined in his genes, but there are some things that I knew had to be removed. So, with the simple step of tell God yes, I was able to destroy and renounce and repent for the unwanted virus that was attacking my bloodline. The change starts with you and like everything else it follows on through.

Mercy

They sat there and played day after day.

I watch them glow as they all join together.

She woke every day and came to my door even when the kids could not come out. She would wait for hours until we all came out.

 She never wanted to leave even when it was late. But she always promised to come back the next day.

What is your name sweet child so dear. She replied its mercy and I was sent here.

My heart paused or skipped a beat. Because it was a manifestation of God mercy that he promised me.

Confirming my safety, my protection, and my shield. Gods' mercy will always, and every day be here.

Faith

Holding on strong to the promises that have been made.

I cannot see which way I am going.

The path seems dark, and the directions seem unclear.

I cannot see whether I am too far or getting near.

The story I read about the widow who child was pronounced dead, but since she was true to her faith he through Jesus was able to rise.

Feeling like I am scrambling and struggling but like Zacchaeus I am making my way to the top of the sycamore tree, just so I can see the provisions of Gods will that was promised to me.

The weight of the world beating me down, unclear voices all around but I have read in the word he is always near.

Blood streaming from my body left on the ground abandoned and alone, blinded by the shadows of my sorrows but I outstretched my arms and a garment I touched.

Filled with a wind and cool rush of water, I was then healed because he said my faith made me whole.

Many times, I have cried and baked my last cake and inside I died but God's plan is not done, so the oil keeps pouring in.

No matter what I do it seems like evil is all I see, but inside I trust that greater is he who is within me.

Daily we walk through the valley and shadows of death, but if we listen to our heart and follow the light that is on the path beneath our feet, we will never face defeat.

All we need to do is believe with the mustard seed size of our mind, when we hear Gods word which gives us the birth of what we call FAITH!!!

Don't Get Comfortable

All my life I have always been told when you go to family houses, when you go to people's houses, and I am saying if y'all are cool like; you like them it is OK to get comfortable.

I have always been taught. I have always been told like; it is OK. You know my house is your house, you know get comfortable.

I have always been told that I do not know if that's a southern thing. That is why I don't never take my shoes off even if they have got that carpet and everybody's shoes lined up, I still walk right on in with mines or I don't come over anymore.

 I do not know if it is a generational thing. I do not know if it is a cultural thing. However, I've always been taught to get comfortable so now it's weird.

I thought about all the times where I was supposed to be comfortable and all the times that I have gotten comfortable and all the times that someone made me feel comfortable and all those times were, I may even thought that it was OK to be comfortable , all those times talk about like every time, I've been kicked down, cast out, cursed out, done wrong, singled out, taken advantage of, hurt in more ways than one and pushed out so I just feel as though and I was just sitting here thinking about it.

Do I want my kids to go to somebody's house just because they know them or just because they are cool with them or just because they gave them the illusion that it was OK to be comfortable do, I really want them to get comfortable.

Their comfort is with their mom at home. Their peace is a spirit that is attached to them. They know that is the one place you can always be comfortable even still you cannot be that comfortable. Some people may not have the comfort of even their mother's home.

I have learnt many things due to those things just sitting here and just allowing these thoughts to come to my forefront because I asked God Show me everything that I need to change, destroy, cast out and come out of agreement with the things that are not of you.

I was sitting here, and God said to me when you get comfortable on your own without me telling you it is OK to be comfortable then that comfort is gone soon come to an end It's going to soon create a problem.

It is going to soon hurt your feelings, going to soon make you cry. It has gone soon break your heart that getting comfortable on your own. It does a lot of damage to you so I sit here, and he just broke It all the way down and listening to him break it down I understood no, I would never teach them to always be comfortable not, so it is OK. It is OK to love. It is OK to like a place. It is OK to love a place, it is OK to like a job. It is OK to love a job. It is OK to love a lot of things. It is OK to like them That is perfectly fine.

Do not get comfortable. If you are comfortable, you are not allowing room for growth, transformation, and the end of your season. You do not want to put a limit of the abundance that God has for you. You do not want to bury the many talents God has put inside of you. If God do not tell you to get comfortable, then do not, he said he will give you a sweet sleep.

When you get comfortable you take off your shoes, kick your feet up and even lay across their beds. You sit in their presence and share your secrets. You sit in their presence and let your guard that is around your heart come down. just even by getting comfortable in your career if it does not align with your purpose, you will still get the same results especially if God did not say this is your end place.

But you might like it, so this was a perfect lesson a perfect teaching, perfect instructions. Perfectly he said present ideas to him. Will you put it in the master hands? That is the one, so how you going to get comfortable Do not ever get comfortable, naturally, emotionally, or even spiritually until God tells you that you're comfortable for anything and anywhere.

Speak to Me

Speak to me father so I don't have to stare.

Speak to me father even though I may not be prepared.

Speak to me father, I know you are there.

Speak to me father because you are the only one that cares.

Speak to me father I am seeking your face.

Speak to me father and fill the empty space.

Speak to me father and let me know everything is all right.

Speak to me father so I can stop having sleepless nights.

Speak to me father so this heavy heart can be light.

Speak to me father, please just come hold me tight.

Speak to me father I am crying inside.

Speak to me father so I do not feel like I have died.

Speak to me father even though I feel no pain.

Speak to me father and tell me I am not insane.

Speak to me father my stomach is turning.

Speak to me father, I am not sure if I am rightly discerning.

Speak to me father, I love and need you.

Speak to me father because I know you love me to.

Speak to me father because my battles are not mine.

Speak to me father please tell me what is next in line.

Speak to me father you are the only one I trust.

Speak to me father cause following you is a must.

Speak to me father this silence I dread.

Speak to me father, I know there is more to be said.

Speak to me father, would you rather me shout?

Speak to me father one way or another it has to come out.

Speak to me father about the things I see and the feelings I have.

Speak to me father, I need assurance I am on the right path.

Speak to me father I long for our one-on-one talks.

Speak to me father simply because ahead of me you walk.

Speak to me father, I am your baby you see.

Speak to me father because you are the one who ordained me.

Speak to me father while I am awake or sleep.

Speak to me father so my heart can again leap.

Speak to me father I need a divine release.

Speak to me father, cause when you do, I am at peace.

A Prophets Cry

Tears not seen that are deep inside.

Tears that flow but not from your eyes.

Tears that would usually make your heart hurt.

Tears that fill you with a sick stuffed feeling.

Tears that drip even when your mind is blank.

Tears that make the strongest heart sank.

Tears that swell you up like a balloon.

Tears that have you wondering will it end soon.

Tears that seem to come with every season.

Tears that fill up and pour out for no reason.

Tears that go on more than the rains of Noah days.

Tears that have you stuck in an endless daze.

Tears that take every breath away.

Tears that have you choke in many ways.

Tears of joy and sometimes pain.

Tears that have even the wise feeling insane.

Tears that drown everything out.

Tears that cause a loud deep inside shout.

Tears that are intense and dreadfully strong.

Tears that have you wondering if you did something wrong.

Tears that only God knows why.

Tears that cannot be wiped because they do not come from the eye.

Tears that make you bow down and pray.

Tears that wash soon are gone by day.

Tears that come from endless hate.

Tears that come from you having to tell people their fate.

Tears that come from what would make normal people scared.

Tears that come but God constantly remind you that you are prepared.

Tears that are sometimes not for you.

Tears that rain because visions of the world being a wild zoo.

Tears that express helplessness because there is nothing you can do.

Tears that come because what God shows you.

Calling on my life

There has been a calling on my life, apparently before the world was formed.

Theres been a calling on my life, my mother was not aware. Because if she were, she would have protected me better.

Theres been a calling on my life to set some captives free, but looking at my life I wonder how me?

Theres been a calling on my life to break generational curses. But I have opened some doors of my own and allowed some things in my home.

There has been a calling on my life that interrupts my sleep, I see even the deepest things people hide.

There has been a calling on my life that scared me from the age of 5, but a prophet like me was called at just 8.

There is a calling on my life I did not understand, but he sent the Holy Spirit to teach me all things.

There is a calling on my life to intercede for many, even the ones who damaged and scared me had to be forgiven.

There is a calling on my life I did not even ask for, but it's for me to do so I can't pass it to you.

There is a calling on my life that came with talents, I hid the box and almost lost them all.

There is a calling on my life that does not make since, but God promised he will never leave or forsake me.

There is a calling on my life kind of like Noah you know the one with the ark, but first God said he had to give me a new heart.

There is a calling on my life that at times it's dark, but God sent a word to be a lamp and guide my feet and light my path.

There is a calling on my life even though evil and sin is always with me. I just keep a heart like David and stay repenting.

There is a calling on my life with this rage that Moses had, but just like Joseph, I will make it to the promise land.

There is a calling on my life that makes me a huge target, but he has this secret place that he keeps me hidden in.

There is a calling on my life a job I'm unsure that I can do.

But there are many stories told of how with him we always made it through.

Theres a calling on my life I don't know how to start or even when and where it will end. But I gave my yes, and I chose to dive right in.

THE END

Synopsis:

A Glance in My Heart is a deeply moving collection of poems that explores the spiritual battles faced by a woman chosen by God. Through raw and honest reflections, the poems capture the highs and lows of her journey, offering solace and inspiration to women who feel alone in their struggles. Through the tapestry of her words, she reveals the depths of her spiritual battles, sharing the moments of strength, doubt, and divine grace that have shaped her path. This collection is a testament to the resilience of the human spirit and a reminder that no woman is ever truly alone, as God's love and understanding are always present. Each poem serves as a comforting voice, encouraging readers to find strength in their faith. This collection is more than just poetry; it is a lifeline for those who are silently enduring, offering comfort, understanding, and the powerful reminder that every woman, no matter how isolated she feels, is part of a greater sisterhood bound by faith and resilience.

About the Author

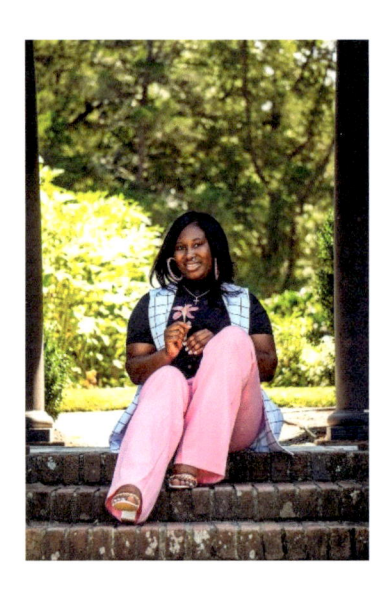

Delicia, an author from Winston-Salem and mother of three, rediscovered her passion for writing in May 2024 after a profound conversation with God about her life's purpose. With God's guidance, she created this book, which reflects not only her personal experiences but also those faced by countless women and even some men every day. Her writing is inspired by a desire to help readers build confidence in God, deepen their faith, and find the strength to persevere through life's challenges. Delicia believes that everyone has a unique purpose, and through prayer, they can discover their own path.

Made in the USA
Columbia, SC
14 September 2024

51ca15f1-ba8b-4b9a-a769-66fa72742f4eR01